Watching the Sun

By Edana Eckart

Welcome Books™

Children's Press®
A Division of Scholastic Inc.
New York / Toronto / London / Auckland / Sydney
Mexico City / New Delhi / Hong Kong
Danbury, Connecticut

Photo Credits: Cover, p. 7 © Alexander Walter/Getty Images; p. 9 © Getty Images; p. 13 © Chris Ladd/Getty Images; pp. 5, 15 © Corbis; p. 11 © Mark M. Lawrence/Corbis; p. 17 © D. Boone/Corbis; p. 19 © Ron Watts/Corbis; p. 21 © Matthias Kulka/Corbis
Contributing Editors: Shira Laskin and Jennifer Silate
Book Design: Michelle Innes

Library of Congress Cataloging-in-Publication Data

Eckart, Edana.
    Watching the sun / by Edana Eckart.
    p. cm.—(Watching nature)
    Summary: Simple text introduces facts about the sun.
    Includes bibliographical references and index.
    ISBN 0-516-27597-6 (lib. bdg.) ISBN 0-516-25939-3 (pbk.)
    1. Sun—Juvenile literature. [1. Sun.] I. Title.

    QB521.5.E25 2004
    523.7—dc21

                                                    2003009114

Contents

It is very early in the
morning.

The Sun is not up yet.

5

Now, it is **dawn**.

The Sun is **rising**.

The Sun rises in the sky all morning.

The sky gets brighter as the Sun rises.

9

At **noon**, the Sun is at its highest place in the sky.

The Sun is bright during the day.

People wear **sunglasses** to keep their eyes safe from the Sun.

13

The Sun makes Earth warm.

It is warmest in the summer.

We can go swimming
when it is warm.

The Sun **sets** in the **evening**.

The sky turns many colors before the Sun sets.

17

The sky gets darker as the Sun goes down.

Soon, the sky will be dark.

19

It is night.

The Sun will rise again tomorrow morning.

New Words

dawn (**dawn**) the beginning of the day when
the Sun can first be seen in the sky

evening (**eev**-ning) the part of the day that
comes after the afternoon but before night

noon (**noon**) twelve o'clock in the middle
of the day

rising (**rize**-ing) going up, moving up, or
getting up

sets (**sets**) the Sun going down as day
becomes night

sunglasses (**suhn**-glass-iz) dark glasses that
protect your eyes from the bright Sun

To Find Out More

Books
The Sun
by Seymour Simon
William, Morrow and Company

The Sun: Our Nearest Star
by Franklyn Mansfield Branley
HarperCollins Children's Books

Web Site
Kids' Adventures in Space
http://www.stargazers.freeserve.co.uk
Read about the Sun, stars, and planets on this Web site
and play fun games.

Index

About the Author

Edana Eckart has written several children's books. She enjoys bike riding with her family.

Reading Consultants

Kris Flynn, Coordinator, Small School District Literacy, The San Diego County Office of Education

Shelly Forys, Certified Reading Recovery Specialist, W.J. Zahnow Elementary School, Waterloo, IL

Paulette Mansell, Certified Reading Recovery Specialist, and Early Literacy Consultant, TX